FATHER & DAUGHTER
PHOTO

THE THREE WEAVERS

Plus Companion Guide

Robert and Shelley Noonan

Pumpkin Seed
P R E S S
Humphrey, Nebraska 68642

All scripture quotations marked NKJ, are taken from the New King James Version, 1979,1980,1982, Thomas Nelson Inc., Publishers. Scripture quotations marked KJV are from The Holy Bible, King James Version 1977,1984, Thomas Nelson Inc., Publishers. All scripture quotations marked NIV are taken from the New International Version 1973,1978,1984 by International Bible Society.

Cover by Annie Tichenor of Tichenor Design Lawrence, Kansas
Painting by J.W. Waterhouse entitled The Lady Of Shalott, 1894.
Packaged by Pine Hill Graphics

Revised and expanded from the original edition in *The Little Colonel* written by Annie Fellows Johnston © 1904

ISBN 0-9700273-5-4

For more information or to order additional copies please contact:
Pumpkin Seed Press LLC,
43668 355th Avenue, Humphrey, Nebraska 68642
(402) 923-1682
www.pumpkinseedpress.net

Pumpkin Seed
P R E S S

Printed in the United States of America.

I will sing of your love and justice;
to you, O LORD, I will sing praise.
I will be careful to lead a blameless life—
when will you come to me?
I will walk in my house
with a blameless heart.
I will set before my eyes
no vile thing.
The deeds of faithless men I hate;
they will not cling to me.
Men of perverse heart shall be far from me;
I will have nothing to do with evil.

(Psalm 101:1-4 NIV)

CONTENTS

FOREWORD

The Three Weavers is actually an excerpt from Chapter 14 of a well known book called *The Little Colonel* by Annie Fellows Johnston published in July of 1903. She wrote a story within a story that was so powerful it still is told today!

Mrs. Johnston was an accomplished author of juvenile fiction from 1890 until 1931. Millions of copies of her books were sold and translated into over 40 languages. Her wholesome, sentimental manner of writing and her strong emphasis on teaching has had a tremendous impact on the young lives it shaped in the last century.

This book is an allegory. An allegory is a representation of abstract ideas or principles by characters in a story form. In this story, Mrs. Johnston has taken great pains to craft a tale that has many layers of truth. There are subtle warnings to be heeded by fathers and daughters alike. Examples abound on the way a father should train and guard his daughter in the area of purity. *The Three Weavers* brings forth truth that can easily and effectively be communicated to young minds of this century as well.

It is our prayer that fathers can use this story and companion material to train, mold and guard their daughters to help them become the women God intends them to be.

HOW TO USE THIS BOOK

GENERAL GUIDANCE

The Three Weavers Plus Companion Guide is intended to be a tool for fathers to mentor their daughters between the ages of nine to sixteen. The allegory begins with the birth of three daughters and ends with the arrival of their "promised princes."

Father, read the entire story to yourself. Then, choose a time each week when you and your daughter can meet. It should take approximately seven weeks; six weeks to complete the study and one week to plan and perform the Purity Ceremony.

1. Look at your calendar and choose seven weeks when you can set aside several hours to undertake this study. Pick a day and a time to begin. Meeting at a set day and time each week creates a clearly marked goal that will be easier to attain.
2. Begin with prayer, asking the Lord to give you a goal for this study. Is it a closer relationship? Do you want to convey to your daughter the importance of remaining pure for marriage? Do you want to set the standard for her future mate? Each time you meet, ask the Lord to guide you. (Psalm 25:4-5)

11

3. Expect God to do great things in your relationship! (Ephesians 3:20)

4. Have a picture taken of you and your daughter. Fasten it to the front of this book that is especially made for this purpose. It will serve as a reminder of the time you spent together.

The first time that you and your daughter meet, be familiar enough with the book to give her a sneak peek at what you'll be doing together. Tell her that you will be working on items for her hope chest or hope box; there will be father and daughter dates, Bible studies, and letters of promise that you will exchange. Your six-week study will end with a purity ceremony in which she will receive a gift as a reminder of her promise to remain pure for her marriage to the promised "prince."

COMPANION PORTIONS

Each chapter includes the story, discussion guide, a Bible study for the fathers, and an activity section.

Story:

The Three Weavers has six chapters. Each time you meet you will read one chapter. You may want to begin your study by reading the story in its entirety to your daughter the first time you meet.

Discussion Questions:

Discussion questions will help father and daughter talk about and explore the deeper meaning of the allegory and apply it to their lives. These times of discussion can open up greater understanding into the way your daughter thinks and reacts to different situations.

Hope Chest:

You'll need a hope chest or hope box to hold three letters you'll write, a gift for your daughter to open on her wedding day, and other possessions she treasures. You may prefer to purchase one from your local antique store or from Hope Chest Legacy (see page 131), an on-line store that specializes in Hope Chests. Hobby stores in your area may also carry decorative boxes that could be used for this purpose.

Father's Bible Study:

How can we discover God's purpose for our lives, and gain insight on how to live a life pleasing to God? By reading the Word. After the Discussion Guide in each chapter, there is a Father's Bible Study section to complete *before* your time with your daughter.

God's Word has much to say about fatherhood and the art of guarding a daughter's heart! On what does the Lord want you to focus as you do this study together? If you are not certain or don't understand something cry out to God in prayer. He promises, *"Call to Me and I will answer you and show you great and mighty things, you do not know."* (Jeremiah 33:3 NIV)

The Father's Bible Study section was created to help you discover what God says about sex within marriage and how to present this to your daughter, examine what kind of father you are, evaluate the mistakes the characters in the story made, recognize personality traits in your daughter that may make it difficult to guard her heart, and point out character traits to develop in your daughter to make it easier to guard her heart.

Activities:

Enriching exercises to enhance your experience together are suggested in this section. This part should be fun and meaningful for both of you.

Purity Ceremony:

This can be as involved or as simple as you and your wife choose. The poem on page 129 may be read to your daughter at the ceremony. Pages 131 and 132 have a list of companies that specialize in meaningful gifts for this occasion.

Aim Enterprises is a company we can personally recommend. They have designed a ring that would be a beautiful keepsake to present during the Purity Ceremony. The *"Key to My Heart"* ring includes a heart shaped ring with birthstone and a keyhole in the center. Also included is a tie-tack/ lapel pin for the father that is in the shape of a key. See page 131 for contact information.

THE PLAN

Before you start:

❏ Set aside a time each week for seven weeks to study The Companion Guide to The Three Weavers with your daughter. (If you are involved in another Bible study you may want to consider postponing it so you can give your daughter your full attention.)

❏ Read the story on your own and familiarize yourself with the activities that you will be doing with your daughter.

❏ Complete the Father's Bible Study for chapter 1 and do the activity: to write a letter to your daughter about the day she was born.

❏ With your wife, start preparations for the Purity Ceremony to be held at the conclusion of this study. See pages 131 and 132 for companies that specialize in jewelry to commemorate this special occasion.

Week 1

❏ On the day and time you have selected read your daughter the first chapter of the story and answer the discussion questions together.

❏ When you are finished, give her a hope chest or hope box and read to her the letter you wrote about the day she was born.

Week 2

❑ Before you meet, complete the Father's Bible Study for chapter 2.

❑ Select, purchase and wrap a present you would like your daughter to wear on her wedding day.

❑ Read your daughter the second chapter of the story and answer the discussion questions together.

❑ Read "The Present" aloud and give her the wrapped present to keep unopened until her wedding day. Place it in her hope chest or hope box.

Week 3

❑ Before you meet, complete the Father's Bible Study for chapter 3.

❑ Read the example and write your own "Silver Yardstick Letter."

❑ Read your daughter the third chapter of the story and answer the discussion questions together.

❑ Read your letter aloud and ask her to write her *"Letter of Promise"* to you. Give her a few days. You may want to have these letters framed or put them in the hope chest or box.

Week 4

❑ Before you meet, complete the Father's Bible Study for chapter 4.

❑ Make a list of topics you want to talk about with your daughter.

❑ Read your daughter the fourth chapter of the story and answer the discussion questions together.

❑ Choose and talk about some of the things that are on your list of important things to talk about.

Week 5

❑ Before you meet, complete the Father's Bible Study for chapter 5.

❑ Write your daughter a letter in which you promise to always look out for her good in every decision that you make.

❑ Read your daughter the fifth chapter of the story and answer the discussion questions together.

❑ Read her your letter giving your pledge so she'll know that she can always count on you to have her best at heart.

Week 6

❑ Before you meet, complete the Father's Bible Study for chapter 6.

❑ Plan a Purity Ceremony.

❑ Read your daughter the sixth chapter of the story and answer the discussion questions together.

Week 7

❑ Plan and perform the Purity Ceremony with your daughter.

THE LADY OF SHALOTT

Based on the poem by
Lord Alfred Tennyson
(1809-1892)

There she weaves by night and day
A sacred¹web with colours gay.
She has heard a whisper say,
A curse is on her if she stay
To look down to Camelot.
She knows not what the curse may be,
And so she weaveth steadily,
And little other care hath she,
The Lady of Shalott.

And moving across a window² clear
That hangs before her all the year,
Shadows of the world appear.
There she sees the highway near
Winding down to Camelot:
There the river eddy whirls,
And there the surly village-churls,
And the red cloaks of market girls,
Pass onward from Shalott.

Sometimes a troop of damsels glad,
An abbot on an ambling pad,
Sometimes a curly shepherd-lad,
Or long-hair'd page in crimson clad,
Goes by to tower'd Camelot;
And sometimes thro' the mirror blue
The knights come riding two and two:
She hath no loyal knight and true,
The Lady of Shalott.

---

1. Magic was the word used in the original work of Tennyson
2. Mirror was used in the original.

THE THREE FAMILIES

*"Their houses stood side by side and their lives were so
similar that whatever good happened under one roof
always happened under the roofs of the others."*

Once upon a time, during the same time that the
Lady of Shalott[3] wove her web, there lived three
weavers. Their houses stood side by side and
their lives were so similar that whatever good thing happened under one roof always happened under the roof of
the others. They wove the same patterns of cloth on their
looms, and they each received the same amount of money
for their webs.[4] They sang the same songs, told the same
tales, ate the same kind of soup from the same kind of
bowls, and dressed in the same coarse goods of an undyed
wool called hodden gray.

However, the three weavers were unlike as three
weavers could possibly be. The first, named Dexter,
insisted upon weaving all his webs to one exact length,
regardless of the size of the man who would wear his
mantle.[5] Each of the webs the weaver wove was to be just
long enough to make exactly one mantle.

---

3. **Lady of Shalott**, an Arthurian woman depicted in a poem by the same name from Lord
   Alfred Tennyson.
4. **Web**, the length of cloth woven in a loom.
5. **Mantle**, a loose sleeveless garment worn over other clothing, a cloak.

The second weaver, Elton, carelessly wove his web in any length that he happened to think was easiest. He would stretch or cut it afterward to make it fit whomever would purchase it. The webs he wove were of many different sizes and shapes, so much so that no two were ever the same.

The third weaver, Griffin, took painstaking care with each of the webs he wove. First he measured the man by the inches and the ells.[6] Then he carefully compared his measurements to the notched silver yardstick that was his constant companion.

---

6. Ell, an old English measure for cloth of about 45 inches.

Chapter One

DISCUSSION GUIDE

The Three Families

**"...they sang the same songs, told the same tales...
and dressed in the same coarse goods of hodden gray."**

1. As you have read through the story you have discovered many ways that the three families were alike. Comment on the similarities of their:

Houses: _____

_____

Occupations: _____

_____

Songs: _____

_____

Food: _____

_____

Tales: _____

_____

Clothing: _____

_____

2. *"But they were unlike as three weavers could possibly be."* The differences between the three weavers' lives are evident in their work and also in the lives of their

daughters. Did each of them do their work differently? Write anything that you have observed about
the work they performed or their attitudes toward
their work.

Weaver #1: Dexter

_____

_____

_____

_____

Weaver #2: Elton

_____

_____

_____

_____

Weaver #3: Griffin

_____

_____

_____

_____

Chapter One
FATHER'S BIBLE STUDY
The Three Families

"God saw all that he had made, and it was very good."
Genesis 1:31a

Even though these three fathers' families had similar occupations, lived in similar locations, and had similar family size and activities, we can see already that the fathers were very different in their approach to their weaving. They responded very differently to guarding their daughters' purity.

Since you have chosen to go through this book with your daughter, you obviously have a desire to train her in this area. As a father, you have the privilege and responsibility of not just telling your daughter what God's law forbids, but of teaching what His heart *was* in giving these commands. When your daughter understands her Heavenly Father's intention, she can obey with understanding, not because she should or must, but because she understands that it is for her own good that these standards were set in place.

BIBLE STUDY:

As you and your daughter progress through this book and cover the concepts on sexual purity, remember that:

1. God made everything, including sex, and called it good.
2. God designed sex to be enjoyed within certain well-prescribed boundaries.
3. God expects us to talk about these issues in a manner which is pleasing to Him and almost always contrary to the world's view.

Look up the following verses to discover God's view on these three points.

God made sex and called it good. While sexual purity may be an uncomfortable subject for fathers to talk about with their daughters, realize that we shouldn't be embarrassed to talk about what God was not embarrassed to create.

1. Genesis 1:31; Genesis 2:24

_____

_____

_____

_____

God designed sex to be enjoyed within the boundaries of marriage.

2. Hebrews 13:4; Proverbs 6:25-33; Titus 2:12-13

_____

_____

_____

_____

God expects us to discuss the subject in a *manner* in keeping with His view, not the world's.

3. Ephesians 5:3-4; Romans 13:13-14

_____

_____

_____

_____

ACTIVITY:

Take a few minutes to travel back in time to the day your daughter was born. What were your first thoughts? What responsibilities did you feel? What were your first moments like together? Write your daughter a letter about how you felt and what you thought of the day she was born.

Read the letter you wrote to your daughter after your Father and Daughter Bible study. Give the letter to her to put in her hope chest. If she doesn't have a hope chest, present her with a beautiful box or even a hope chest in which she can keep the three letters you will be writing her.

Chapter Two

⚜

THE THREE FATHERS
"The three friends rejoiced together…"

Now to each of the three weavers was born a daughter, and all on the same day! As was the custom during that time, the three weavers named their daughters with names that started with the same first letter as in *their* first names. The three new daughters were named Dinah, Esmee, and Gabriella by their fathers.

In the quiet of the evening after the births of their three daughters, the proud fathers sat smoking their pipes on their common stoop. Dexter, the father of Dinah said sheepishly, "Do not think me puffed up with haughty pride, good neighbors, but a wonderful blessing has been given to my family and me today! Clotho, the godly woman who is overseer of the weavers, was present at my Dinah's birth, and left beside her cradle a gift: a tiny loom that from beam[7] to shuttle[8] is of the purest gold. And she whispered to me as she passed by 'God has blessed you

---

7. **Beam**, a wooden cylinder on a loom in which the cloth is wound.
8. **Shuttle**, an instrument that weaves threads between each other.

this day, Dexter! God has promised that He has chosen a prince to wed your daughter.' "

But Dexter's news caused no astonishment to his neighbors. For as you remember, what happened under one roof happened under the roofs of all. The same blessing had been bestowed and the same gift had been left by *each* child's cradle. The three friends rejoiced together and jested about the three king's sons who would one day sit at their tables.

Presently, Griffin, who was the father of Gabriella, said "But there may be a slip 'twixt[9] cup and lip. What happens if our daughters cannot fulfill the conditions required?"

His question hung like a wisp of fog in the cool evening air. At that moment they all three became quiet and thoughtful, for they remembered that Clotho had added in passing, "One thing is necessary. She *must* weave upon this loom that I give her a royal mantle for the prince's wearing. It must be ample and fair to look upon, rich cloth of gold, of princely size and texture. Many will attempt to claim it, but if it is woven rightly the destined prince alone can wear it, and it will fit him as faultlessly as the falcon's feathers fit the falcon.

But, if it *should not* be ample and fine, if it should not be meet for royal wearing, the prince will not deign[10] to don[11] it. The poor maiden's heart shall break, as shattered as the mirror of the Lady of Shalott."

---

9. **Twixt,** betwixt or between.
10. **Deign,** choose
11. **Don,** to wear.

"Oh, well," snorted Dexter when the three had sat in thoughtful silence for a little space, "I will guard against that! I will hide all knowledge of the loom from my daughter, Dinah, until she has grown into womanhood. Then under my watchful eye, by the measurements that I always use, she will weave the perfect garment. In the meantime, she will learn all the arts that are needful for a princess to know—embroidery and fair needlework, and songs upon the lute.[12] But of the weaving she shall not know until she has grown up. I am determined! 'Tis a sorry mess her childish hands would make of it, if to throw the shuttle at a maiden's fickle fancy!"

But Elton shook his head in disagreement. "Why stew about a trifle!" he exclaimed. "Indeed, on such a tiny loom no web of any kind can well be woven. 'Tis but a toy that Clotho left the child to play with, and she will weave her dreams and fancies on it at her own sweet will. I will not interfere! What God has promised God has promised, and I shall do something to change it? Away, friend Griffin, with your forebodings!"

Griffin said nothing in reply but he thought much. He followed the example of the others, and early and late you would have heard the pounding of the three looms. You see, there was a need to work harder than ever now so that the little maidens might have teachers for all the arts becoming a princess—embroidery and fair needlework and songs upon the lute.

---

12. **Lute**, a stringed instrument shaped like a pear.

While the looms pounded in the dwellings the little girls grew apace.[13] They played together in the same garden and learned from the same skilled teachers their daily lessons, and in their fondness for each other they were as close as sisters.

---

13. **Apace**, at a swift pace, quickly.

DISCUSSION GUIDE

The Three Fathers

*"But they were as unlike as three weavers
could possibly be."*

Each of these fathers had a very different interpretation as to what would happen to their daughters if the "required conditions" were not met. Take a deeper look into each father's reaction and the character that is revealed through his actions.

DEXTER, FATHER OF DINAH

*"But of the weaving she shall not know until she has
grown up. I am determined."*

Life Motto: *"Ignorance is bliss"*

1. How would Dexter handle the responsibility of educating his daughter about the golden loom?

_____

_____

_____

_____

_____

2. How was he going to guard her against the knowledge of the loom?

_____

_____

_____

_____

3. By what standards would she be taught to measure the garment that she would someday weave?

_____

_____

_____

_____

4. When was he planning to tell her about the weaving of this special garment?

_____

_____

_____

_____

5. What do you think his rationale was for not explaining the loom to his daughter?

_____

_____

_____

_____

Elton, father of Esmee

"Why stew about a trifle!"
Life Motto: *"Que sera, sera,*
whatever will be, will be..."

1. How would Elton handle the responsibility of educating his daughter about the golden loom?

2. *"Why stew about a trifle!"* What does this statement reveal?

3. In your opinion, what was his reason for not telling his daughter about the weaving of this special garment?

4. Father, has this ever been your attitude? What is your attitude now? Name some of the possible consequences or benefits of this attitude in your daughter's life.

GRIFFIN, FATHER OF GABRIELLA

"But there may be a slip, 'twixt cup and lip. What happens if our daughters cannot fulfill the conditions required?"

Life Motto: "Wait and See"

1. How would Griffin handle the responsibility of educating his daughter about the golden loom?

   _____

   _____

2. What are the only two actions the author tells us he took?

   _____

   _____

3. In your opinion, when do you think Griffin was planning on telling Gabriella about the gift and its special purpose?

   _____

   _____

4. Concerning the gift, Griffin made this insightful comment, *"But there may be a slip, 'twixt cup and lip. What happens if our daughters cannot fulfill the conditions required?"* In your own words, what does this

statement mean and what does it reveal about Griffin's character?

_____

_____

_____

_____

5. Father, has this ever been your attitude?

_____

_____

6. What is your attitude now?

_____

_____

_____

7. Name a few consequences or benefits of this attitude in your daughter's life.

_____

_____

_____

_____

_____

Chapter Two

FATHER'S BIBLE STUDY

The Three Fathers

"While the looms pounded in the dwellings the little girls grew apace."

Do you realize that God also has a very special gift and promise for your daughter? It is the gift of sexual purity. He has designed this gift to be cherished, honored, and kept safely until her wedding day when she gives it to her husband. But in order to keep the gift until that time, *you* must have a plan.

In this section, you will examine the precious gift and promise God has for your daughter and you'll start to think about the plan you will be developing throughout this study.

BIBLE STUDY:

Look up the following verses, write them out and meditate on their meaning in regard to your daughter. Record any insights that the Lord gives you.

The Gift: This good and perfect gift *IS* from God! He has an appropriate time for it to be opened.

• James 1:17

_____

_____

_____

_____

Insight:

_____

_____

_____

_____

The Plan: God has a special plan for your daughter which includes her remaining pure for her future husband.

• Isaiah 25:1

_____

_____

_____

_____

Insight:

_____

_____

_____

_____

God has a particular plan for your daughter's life that has been "formed of old." He already knows the turns, bumps and pitfalls she will face and He has designed the PERFECT plan for her life and yours!

• **Proverbs 16:9**

_____

_____

_____

_____

Insight:

_____

_____

_____

_____

Every father needs a plan of action for protecting and preserving the special gift that God has given his daughter. But even before you create a plan you need to ask the Lord to direct you and to make your plan exactly what He wants. Ultimately, He is in control of all our plans!

The Promise:

• Jeremiah 29:11

_____

_____

_____

_____

Insight:

_____

_____

_____

_____

The Lord's plan for your daughter is for her good!
He is carefully putting it in place to give her hope
and a future.

ACTIVITY:

1. Purchase a gift for your daughter that is not to be opened until her wedding day. Choose carefully something she will want to wear on that special day! She can keep it in her hope chest or hope box and should not open it until the day she is married. The gift does not need to be expensive. A necklace with single pearl or pearl earrings are a good choice. Have the sales attendant or your wife wrap up the gift in beautiful wrapping paper and a bow.

2. Read the story on page 41 to your daughter and discuss it together. Then give her the wrapped present you have purchased for her to wear on her wedding day.

THE PRESENT

Have you ever opened a present before it was time? Once there was a little girl who couldn't wait for Christmas day to arrive because under the tree was a beautifully wrapped package with her name on it.

One day near Christmas when her parents were gone for the whole afternoon, she walked over to the Christmas tree and very carefully opened the present. Inside she found just the doll she had wanted. She played with it all afternoon, then carefully placed it back in its box and re-wrapped the present so it looked as if it hadn't been opened. When Christmas morning arrived she opened her present and acted surprised, but in her heart she was bitterly disappointed...the thrill of the new doll had already been experienced and now the excitement was gone.

Many young women give away their special gift before their wedding day and experience the sadness of not waiting. Dear girl, you too have been given a wonderful gift. That is the gift of having a heart, mind and body to be saved for only the "prince" God has for you.

To remind you of this precious gift that God has given you, I want to give you this present to keep in your hope chest or box until your wedding day. Let this present represent the gift that you are keeping for your husband, a gift you may not open until your wedding day.

Chapter Three

THE THREE DAUGHTERS' DISCOVERY

"Come with me and I will show you a beautiful toy that Clotho left me at my birth."

O ne day Esmee said excitedly to the other girls, "Come with me and I will show you a beautiful toy that Clotho left me at my birth. My father says she gave a golden loom to each of us, and that it was promised that we are each to wed a prince if we can weave for him an ample cloak of gold. Already I have begun to weave mine!"

Silently, for fear of watchful eyes and forbidding voices, they crept into Esmee's inner room and she showed them the loom of gold. But it was no longer a tiny toy that had been left beside the cradle. Amazingly, the loom had grown as Esmee had grown. For every inch that was added to her stature an inch had been added to the loom. The warp[14]

---

14. **Warp**, the threads lengthwise in the loom, crossed by the woof.

included in Clotho's gift, all golden thread, had also grown with the young maiden's growth; but the thread that the shuttle carried was of her own spinning—rainbow hued and rose-colored, from the airy dream fleece of her own sweet fancies.

"See," she whispered, "I have begun the mantle for my prince's wearing." Seizing the shuttle as she had seen her father do many times, she crossed the golden warp with the woof-thread[15] of a rosy daydream. Dinah and Gabriella looked on in silent envy, not so much for the loom as for that which they saw through the window that hung behind the loom. The same young men that sauntered and flitted past theirs, passed outside of Esmee's!

"Look out there!" she cried as she pointed out the window. "Look at that curly haired shepherd lad! Doesn't he look like a prince as he strides by my window with his head held high and his bright blue eyes smiling at all the world? He carries his crook just the way a king would carry a royal scepter. You can understand why I am at my loom from sunrise to sunset to catch a glimpse of him as he passes by."

"Do you see the long-haired page in crimson clothing over on the hill? He is more to my liking," said Dinah timidly. "I-I- think *he* must be of noble blood. He carries himself like one brought up in a palace. I wonder why my father has never said a word to me about Clotho's gift. I,

---

15. **Woof-thread**, the thread that crosses the warp in a woven fabric.

too, should be at my weaving, for I am the same age as you, Esmee!"

"And I, too," added Gabriella.

"Ask your fathers," suggested Esmee. "Perhaps they have forgotten to tell you."

DISCUSSION GUIDE

The Three Daughters' Discovery

"They played together in the same garden and learned from the same skilled teachers their daily lessons, and in their fondness for each other they were as close as sisters."

As the three daughters grew swiftly, their fathers worked even harder than before so their daughters might have all their needs taken care of. The three girls were like sisters in their fondness for each other but they were also very different.

ESMEE, DAUGHTER OF ELTON

"...but the thread the shuttle carried was of her own spinning..."

Nickname: *"Dream Weaver"*

1. Describe how you think Esmee viewed the gift Clotho gave her.

_____

_____

_____

_____

_____

2. In your opinion, do you think she knew what Clotho's promise was? Retell it in your own words.

_____

_____

3. As you remember, there were "required conditions" attached to the promise. Do you believe Esmee was aware of them? Give reasons to support your answer.

_____

_____

_____

_____

4. "*Silently, for fear of watchful eyes and forbidding voices, they crept into an inner room, and she (Esmee) showed them the loom of gold.*" Do you think they were sneaking around? Why do you think they were acting this way?

_____

_____

_____

_____

5. The warp or lengthwise thread in Esmee's loom was made of the golden thread Clotho had given her. The thread that the shuttle carried was of "her own spinning." What color was it?

_____

Using your imagination, make some guesses as to what the color represented.

_____

Speculate on the strength of the garment partially woven of this thread.

_____

_____

_____

_____

6. *"Seizing the shuttle as she had seen her father do so many times…"* Do you think that Esmee's father meant to instruct her how to weave? Why or why not?

_____

_____

_____

7. Dinah and Gabriella seemed envious of Esmee's loom and her window. Give some reasons you think that they felt that way.

_____

_____

_____

8. Whom did Esmee see in her window?

_____

Explain the rationalization she used to describe the shepherd lad as a prince.

_____

_____

_____

9. Have you ever had a crush on someone that may not be God's best for you?

_____

_____

_____

Did you rationalize his manner, appearance, or attitude?

_____

_____

10. An old proverb states: "Bad company corrupts." How did Esmee's attitude "rub off" on Dinah?

_____

_____

_____

_____

11. Rewrite Elton's attitude about the loom and his daughter in your own words.

_____

_____

_____

_____

_____

_____

DINAH, DAUGHTER OF DEXTER

"I wonder why my father has never said a word to me about Clotho's gift."

Nickname: *"Shame Weaver"*

❧⳯❧

1. Esmee had a lot of influence on Dinah. Why do you think she listened to her friend's council?

_____

_____

_____

2. Have you ever had a friend like Esmee?

_____

Describe how she might have influenced you.

_____

_____

_____

3. Whom did Dinah see out of the window?

_____

Explain her rationalization for describing the "long-haired page in crimson clothing" as a prince.

_____

_____

_____

4. Think about a time when your parents told you no, but instead of listening you decided you knew better and did what you wanted anyway! How did the situation turn out?

_____

_____

_____

5. Name any lesson(s) you have learned about your friends and your own personality from Dinah's experiences.

_____

_____

_____

GABRIELLA, DAUGHTER OF GRIFFIN

"Dinah and Gabriella looked on in silent envy, not so much for the loom as for that which they saw through the window that hung behind the loom."

Nickname: *"Weaver Extraordinaire"*

There is hardly anything written about Gabriella in this chapter except when Dinah voiced she should be "at her weaving" because she was the same age as Esmee, Gabriella said "And I, too."

1. Gabriella looked at Esmee's loom and window in silent envy. Speculate why.

   _____

   _____

   _____

   _____

2. Did Gabriella see the same young men that the other two girls saw out of the window? Name them.

   _____

   _____

3. Describe how Dinah and Esmee formed attachments (crushes) with the two young men they saw.

   _____

   _____

   _____

4. Gabriella *did not* form an attachment. Evaluate why you think she didn't and explain what this says about Gabriella's character.

_____

_____

_____

_____

5. Do you get crushes easily?

_____

What are some ways this could be dangerous for you?

_____

_____

_____

_____

6. Discuss with your father methods in which you can "guard your heart" and avoid crushes that might hurt you.

_____

_____

_____

_____

_____

Fathers, now would be a good time to talk to your daughter about what it means to guard your heart.

Chapter Three

FATHER'S BIBLE STUDY

The Three Daughters' Discovery

"They played together in the same garden and learned from the same skilled teachers their daily lessons, and in their fondness for each other they were as close as sisters."

As the three daughters grew swiftly, their fathers worked even harder than before so the daughters might have all their needs taken care of. The three girls were as sisters in their fondness for each other but they were also very different from each other. Each exhibited different character traits that either *contributed* to or were *detrimental* to the guarding of their hearts.

In the following section, you will discover three character traits to cultivate in your daughter to help her effectively guard her heart. The three traits are **Discretion**, **Obedience**, and **Trustworthiness**.

ESMEE, DAUGHTER OF ELTON

"...but the thread the shuttle carried was of her own spinning..."

Nickname: *"Dream Weaver"*

Esmee could be accused of using the spinning of her own thoughts and ideas into the weaving of her coat(s), but perhaps we can excuse her. She had no instruction from her father, so how could she possibly know the correct way?

A strong and convincing argument could be made in defense of this young woman, however, there is an equally strong case to be made that she just plain lacked good judgment. The Bible refers to this desirable character trait as discernment and discretion.

Discernment and discretion are the first qualities your daughter needs to guard her heart. Discernment and discretion are two different qualities, but often confused. **Discernment** is to perceive, to understand a situation in the mind as with the eye, to understand, or to detect. **Discretion** is discernment put into action. It is the exercise of godly judgment in everyday life.

Bible Study:

Read the following verses and answer the questions.

"My son (daughter), if you accept my words and store up my commands within you, turning your ear to wisdom and applying your heart to understanding, and if you call out for insight and cry aloud for understanding, and if you look for it as for silver and search for it as for hidden treasure, then you will understand the fear of the LORD and find the knowledge of God.

Then you will understand what is right and just and fair—every good path. For wisdom will enter your heart, and knowledge will be pleasant to your soul. Discretion will protect you, and understanding will guard you." (Proverbs 2:1-5, 9-11 NIV)

1. According to this passage what is the one key to having discernment?

   _____

   _____

   _____

   _____

2. In the Scripture passage above, underline the seven conditions to gaining discernment.

3. The result of gaining discernment is explained in verses nine and ten. Take time to reread them and write them out in your own words.

_____

_____

_____

_____

4. God promises dads that even when they are not there to protect their daughters...

"Discretion will protect you and understanding will guard you." Proverbs 2:11 NIV

ACTIVITY:

1. Pray right now that the Lord would help you establish a plan to train your daughter in discretion.

2. Using the seven touchstones of discretion outlined in Proverbs 2:1-4 evaluate your daughter's level of discernment. Answer the following questions. Form a plan to help her achieve these goals.
   • Does she accept my words of advice and correction?
   • Is she storing up God's commands in her heart?
   • Does she turn her ear toward wisdom?
   • Have I seen her apply her heart to understand what is right and wrong and why?
   • Am I aware that she is calling out to God in an active and interactive prayer life?
   • Have I noticed that she is looking for understanding as if it were silver or gold?
   • Does she search for wisdom as aggressively as she would search for hidden treasure?

DINAH, DAUGHTER OF DEXTER

"My father is indeed a tyrant...I shall daily steal away
...to weave in secret..."

Nickname: "Shame Weaver"

Poor, poor Dinah. Her father was a tyrant! In chapter 4 you will find that Dinah did the right thing at first ...she went to her father and asked him about the weaving. He harshly forbade her from weaving and tried to belittle and shame her into obedience. Dinah's error came when she chose to weave in secret after he told her not to weave at all. After all, Dinah rationalized, both her friends were doing it! Dinah would be left out if she did not weave her web with the others!

Dinah's life would have been easier and less disappointing if she had just obeyed her father. Severe as he was, God placed him over her to guard her heart and protect her from harm. Dinah would have avoided great pain if she had been obedient to her father's wishes.

Obedience is the *second* trait to cultivate in your daughter's character. This trait is necessary for *her* to have in order for *you* to guard her heart. There will be times when you make a decision that she will see you as a tyrant. Learning to be obedient, even when she doesn't understand your reasons, could save her from untold heartbreak.

Webster defines obedience as "A willingness to obey; to be submissive to restraint, control or command" Find out what Scripture says about obedience and techniques you can use to train your daughter to develop this rare quality.

1. Use your Bible to look up and answer these questions. From where should obedience come?

Deuteronomy 30:2

_____

_____

Romans 6:17

_____

_____

Romans 1:5

_____

_____

_____

How does God see obedience?

1 Samuel 15:22

_____

_____

_____

Describe the correct attitude of obedience.

Psalm119: 34

_____

_____

_____

Isaiah 1:19

_____

_____

_____

Philippians 2:12

_____

_____

_____

Joshua 22:2-3

_____

_____

_____

2. How can you train your daughter in obedience?

Model it. _"In everything set them a good example by doing what is good." (Titus 2:7 NIV)_
Teach it. _"All Scripture is… useful for teaching, rebuking, correcting and training in righteousness." (2 Timothy 3:16 NIV)_
Expect it. _"Train up a child in the way he (she) should go and when he (she) is old, he (she) will not depart from it." (Proverbs 22:6 NKJV)_

ACTIVITY:

Take some time right now to allow the Lord to search your heart and point out any ways you are not being obedient to Him. Repent of them and ask Him for forgiveness. Then, take some time to talk to the Lord on behalf of your daughter. Ask Him to show you ways to train your daughter in obedience. On the lines below, write down what the Lord encourages you to do.

_____

_____

_____

_____

_____

_____

_____

_____

_____

_____

_____

_____

_____

_____

_____

GABRIELLA, DAUGHTER OF GRIFFIN

"…it was promised that we are each to wed a prince if
we can weave for him an ample cloak of gold."

Nickname: *"Weaver Extraordinaire"*

As the story unfolds you will discover that Gabriella and Griffin succeeded. Both of them responded correctly; Gabriella by talking to her father about the discovery of her golden loom and the promise of her future princely husband and Griffin by his gentle response to her questions and loving attitude.

Trustworthiness is the third and perhaps the most important factor in your daughter's character. There must be *mutual trust* in order for there to be success in your relationship: your daughter must trust you and you must in turn trust your daughter.

Mutual Trust = Relationship

Trust on her part means having a faith, reliance, expectation and belief that you indeed have her best interest at heart. Inversely, trust can be defined for you as caring, keeping, protecting and guarding her and desiring her very best. Ultimately, your trust relationship with her will form her view of her heavenly Father. You have a weighty responsibility.

ACTIVITY:

The following activities will help develop deeper trust between the two of you. One is for you and one is for your daughter.

1. Write a *Silver Yardstick Letter,* outlining the **measurements** and **qualities** you want her future husband to have. All the men she considers for her future husband should be held up to this standard.

   The letter on page 65 is an example. Read it, then create your own! You may prefer to adapt the letter on page 65, adding or subtracting items. Be prepared to explain any of the points to your daughter. Your points need to be based on scripture so you can fortify your position with biblical truth.

Dear _____,

This letter is our Silver Yardstick Letter for you to use to measure any man who comes into your life and wants to be your husband.

1. He must be a Christian, walking with the Lord. 2 Corinthians 6:14; 1 Corinthians 9:24; Ephesians 5:1-2
2. You must be willing to trust him and be willing to submit to his authority in your home. 1 Peter 3:1-7
3. He must be capable of supporting a family.
4. Both of you must have similar life goals.
5. He must meet with my approval.

Please know that I treasure you and I have your very best interest at heart in all the actions that I do. I look forward to the life God has planned for you with the very special "prince" He has chosen just for you.

Love,
Dad

P.S. Let's read this together on the eve of your wedding celebration!

2. After you have finished writing your own version of the *Silver Yardstick Letter* complete the following activity with your daughter. Have your daughter write a **"Letter of Promise,"** her pledge to you to confirm the man she chooses is from God.

Choose a time after the reading of this section and your discussion to give each other the letters. These letters may be placed in her hope chest to be read and re-read as time passes as a reminder of the standards you have set for her future "prince" and of the promise she made you to wait until she is married to give herself to her husband. You might even want to frame both letters and hang them in a prominent place so she can read them over and over.

Read the message on page 67 with your daughter to explain about the letter you want her to write. Give her a set amount of time to write it.

In your life, you will have many boys who will come to you and say with honeyed words, "I am the one that God has destined for you!" But do not let them persuade you to give your heart to them. I want you to be able to talk to me about them; I want to be able to guide you and guard you through these times in your life because I love you dearly and only want the best for you. I am asking you to write a letter to me giving your promise to allow me to guard you.

Trust is a two way street. You need to trust me to have your best interest at heart, and I need to be able to trust that you will seek my advice on this matter and allow me to ask tough questions about any relationship you are in.

Take time now to write a letter to me. It can be as simple or as complicated as you want it! In the next chapter, this is the promise Gabriella gave to her father. "You may trust me, Father; I will not cut the golden warp from out of the loom until I, a grown woman, have woven such a web as you yourself will say is worthy of my prince's wearing."

Daughter, take time to write your father your "Letter of Promise."

- Mark on your calendar a special time when you will exchange the letters that you have written to each other, such as at a meal in a nice restaurant, over ice cream or on a picnic. Whatever you choose, make it special!

- At the end of this time, pray together. Ask God to preserve the level of trust you have together. Pray for your future son-in-law. Then place the letters in her hope chest or hope box.

Chapter Four

THE FATHERS' REACTIONS

"I have often looked forward to this day, my little one..."

When Dinah reached her home she went directly to her father, Dexter, and said timidly with a soft voice, eyes downcast and cheeks flaming, "Father, wh-where is m-my loom, like Esmee's? I, too, should be weaving a cloak for my promised prince."

Dexter glowered and looked grimly at his daughter. "Who told you this?" he demanded so sternly her timid heart quaked within her. "Hear me!" he roared. "Never again must you listen to such idle tales. When you are a grown woman you may come to me, and I will speak with you then about webs and weavings. What business do you have thinking about such things now? You, a silly little girl! Bah! I am ashamed that a daughter of mine would even think of such foolishness!"

Dinah, shamed, humiliated and confused, stole away to her bedroom to weep. She had been deeply hurt by her father's scorn. The next day when the three girls played in the garden Esmee said, "Your father is an old tyrant to forbid you the use of Clotho's gift. He cannot love you as much as *my* father loves *me*, or he would not deny you such pleasure. Come with me! I will help you find it!"

Hand in hand they stole into Dinah's inner room that Dexter thought he had securely bolted. They found a loom like Esmee's and above it was a window through which the maiden might look at the outside world as she wove. As Dinah picked up the shuttle to send the thread of a rosy daydream through the warp of gold, the longhaired page in bright crimson clothing sauntered past her window.

"How like a prince he bears himself!" she murmured. "My father is indeed a tyrant to deny me the pleasure of looking out upon the world and weaving sweet fancies about it. From now on," she vowed, "I will not obey him. Rather, I will sneak away daily into this room to weave in secret what he will not allow me to do openly."

At the same time, Gabriella stood before her father saying timidly, "Is it true my, father, what Esmee says is promised to me? Today after I saw Esmee's loom I pushed back the bolt that has always barred the door into an inner room, and there I found a loom of gold and a beautiful window. I fain[16] would use it

---

16. **Fain**, to be well pleased or glad.

as Esmee does, but I have come to ask you first if all is well."

A tender smile lighted the face of old Griffin. Taking the hand of young Gabriella in his, he led the way to the inner room.

"I have often looked forward to this day, my little one," he exclaimed, "although I did not think you would come quite so soon with your questions. What Esmee told you has been promised by God about your future is true. And this promise not only affects you, but those who come after you as well."

"'Tis a dangerous gift the good Clotho left you, for looking out the window above your loom you will be tempted to weave your web to fit the shifting figures that flit[17] past it. But listen to me, my daughter; listen to your father who has never deceived you. I only have your good at heart. Keep always by your side this sterling yardstick that I give you now, for it marks the inches and the ells to which the stature of your promised prince *must* be measured. Not until your web is fully equal to the specified measurements can it safely be taken from the loom." Griffin paused and looked intently at Gabriella's face.

"You are so young," Griffin sighed wistfully. "It is only a little mantle that you could weave this year, even if you did your very best. It would only be fit to clothe the shoulders of yon curly shepherd lad." He pointed out the window to the bright reflection passing by on the cobblestone

---

17. **Flit**, to pass by in a quick and darting manner.

street below. "But this is a special loom that lengthens with your growth, and each year the web will grow longer until at last, a grown woman, you can hold it up and compare the web to the silver yardstick and discover if the golden mantle measures up to the last inch and ell of the very size required by a prince's noble stature."

"My dear daughter, I must give warning. You will often be dazzled by the sights out of the windows. The young men will come to you, one by one, each begging you, 'Give *me* the royal mantle, Gabriella! I am the prince God has destined for you!' With honeyed words each will show you how the mantle in the loom is just the perfect length to fit his shoulders. But do not let him persuade you to cut it loose and give it to him, no matter how much you may want to. Weave on another year, and yet another, till you are a grown woman and can measure out the perfect web, more ample than these young men can carry, a mantle that is fitting of your promised prince. This mantle, my daughter, will fit your prince as faultlessly as a falcon's feathers fit the falcon."

Gabriella, awed by her father's words of solemn warning, took the silver yardstick and hung it by the window so that it would be a reminder to her of the true measurements her promised prince must live up to. She then stood before old Griffin with her head bowed and said, "You may trust me, Father; I will not cut the golden warp from out of the loom until I, a grown woman, have woven such a web as you, yourself, will say is worthy of my prince's wearing." So Griffin left her with his blessing, and went back to his work.

After that, winter followed autumn and summer followed spring many times, as the three daughters played in the garden and learned their lessons of embroidery, fair needlework and songs upon the lute. And every day each stole away to her inner room to throw the shuttle in and out among the threads of gold.

DISCUSSION GUIDE

The Fathers' Reactions

"A tender smile lighted the face of old Griffin"

DINAH, DAUGHTER OF DEXTER

"My father is indeed a tyrant…I shall daily sneak away …to weave in secret…"

Nickname: "Shame Weaver"

1. Dinah went to speak to her father about the loom "with eyes downcast and cheeks flaming." What does this tell you about Dinah's personality?

   _____

   _____

   _____

2. Do you think she approached him in a correct way? Why or why not?

   _____

   _____

3. Dexter "glowered and looked grimly upon her." What did he say to her?

_____

_____

_____

4. Imagine how Dinah might have felt. Write it down here.

_____

_____

_____

5. Describe how his attitude influenced Dinah's view of the gift Clotho gave her.

_____

_____

_____

6. "Hand in hand they stole into Dinah's inner room which Dexter thought he had securely bolted..." Why had Dexter bolted the door?

_____

_____

_____

_____

7. The warp or lengthwise thread in Dinah's loom was made of the golden thread Clotho had given her. The thread that the shuttle carried was of "the thread of a rosy daydream." What do you think this thread represents?

_____

_____

_____

_____

_____

8. Again, speculate on the strength of Dinah's garment that was partially woven of this thread.

_____

_____

_____

_____

9. Do you think Dinah was aware of the required conditions attached to the promise? Give reasons for your answers.

_____

_____

_____

_____

_____

Gabriella, daughter of Griffin

*"Is it true, my father, what Esmee says is promised
to me?"*

Nickname: *"Weaver Extraordinaire"*

1. How did Gabriella approach her father? What does
   this tell you about her?

   _____

   _____

   _____

   _____

2. "A tender smile lighted the face of old Griffin." How
   would you describe his reaction to Gabriella's question?

   _____

   _____

   _____

3. Rewrite in your own words what Griffin said to
   Gabriella.

   _____

   _____

   _____

   _____

4. Imagine how Gabriella felt and record it here. In your description, describe how her father's reaction to her questions influenced Gabriella's view of the golden gift.

_____

_____

_____

_____

_____

_____

5. Do you think Gabriella was aware of the "required conditions" attached to the promise? Give reasons to support your answer.

_____

_____

_____

_____

6. Although the three girls were as close as sisters, who had the primary influence on Gabriella's life and what motivated her to listen and heed this advice?

_____

_____

_____

_____

7. The first warning wise Griffin gave his daughter was: "This promise not only affects you, but those who come after you as well." Why would the future happiness of others depend on it? To whom could Griffin have been referring?

_____

_____

_____

_____

_____

8. Repeat Griffin's second warning and the solution he offered.

_____

_____

_____

_____

9. Griffin explained that she could only weave a mantle for the shoulders of the "curly shepherd lad" at that time, but that as Gabriella grew so would her loom. With each passing year the mantle she was weaving would become larger in size to accommodate a prince's noble stature. How does this advice help you understand how to handle the "crushes" you may be experiencing?

_____

_____

_____

10. List the warning(s) that Griffin gave his daughter.

_____

_____

_____

_____

11. What was the promised outcome for Gabriella if she did everything her father had told her?

_____

_____

_____

_____

_____

12. Rewrite Gabriella's solemn promise to her father.

_____

_____

_____

_____

_____

_____

_____

_____

Chapter Four
FATHER'S BIBLE STUDY
The Fathers' Reaction
*"Taking the hand of little Gabriella in his, he led the
way to the inner room."*

Each of the fathers had a unique way that he wove his webs. Frequently the manner in which a father performs his work reveals the same manner in which he trains his daughter.

In the next section, you will explore the ways each man did his work, what this revealed about his character and how it influenced the way he reacted to his daughter's discovery.

It is interesting to note that the way each father viewed the gift influenced the way his daughter would view her gift in the future. Examine yourself through each of the three profiles to see if it could be you. This portion of the study is primarily intended to help you examine the way you "father" your daughter; share your discoveries with her at your discretion.

DEXTER, FATHER OF DINAH

"But of the weaving she shall know naught until she be grown. That I am determined upon."

Life Motto could have been: "Ignorance is bliss"

Dexter was a rigid man. He insisted on weaving all his webs to the exact same length regardless of the purchaser's size. When his daughter asked him about Clotho's gift he became incensed! He had a plan and would not move either to the right or the left of that plan. He cared more for his plan than for his daughter's feelings or his relationship with her!

Webster's dictionary defines someone who is rigid as one who is *"stiff, unyielding, firm, one who is not lax or indulgent but strict."* When a person is unyielding, he often becomes angry and harsh when his plans are changed or alterations need to be made.

BIBLE STUDY:

"A patient man has great understanding, but a quick-tempered man displays folly." Proverbs 14:29 NIV

1. What does this verse say about a man who is patient and about the man who is quick-tempered?

_____

_____

2. Which one are you?

_____

_____

_____

3. Read the following verses and discover the harvest anger reaps. Note the encouraged positive response as well.

"A soft answer turns away wrath, but a harsh word stirs up anger." Proverbs 15:1 NKJV

"And you, fathers, do not provoke your children to wrath, but bring them up in the training and admonition of the Lord." Ephesians 6:4 NKJV

"Fathers, do not provoke your children, lest they become discouraged." Colossians 3:21 NKJV

ACTIVITY:

Dexter focused on rules rather than relationship. If you are a man who is rigid and unyielding, you may have hurt your relationship with your daughter by harsh and angry words. Confess this to the Lord and then, if you feel led, confess your sin to your daughter. *"If we confess our sins, he is faithful and just and will forgive us our sins and purify us from all unrighteousness. If we claim we have not sinned, we make him out to be a liar and his word has no place in our lives."* *(1 John 1:9-10 NIV)*

Your relationship with your daughter will be restored and will be able to grow again. *(Acts 3:19)* Here are some relationship building activities to cultivate a stronger relationship with your daughter.

RELATIONSHIP BUILDERS

1. Take your daughter out on a monthly date when she can spend time alone with her Daddy. For breakfast, lunch, or even just ice cream! (Make sure you date your wife too!)

2. Go window-shopping. This is a great way for you to teach her your standards on modest clothing, training her in what is acceptable to wear and what isn't.

3. Make time each day to ask about her day. What happened that was good? What happened that wasn't good?

4. Tuck her in bed at night. Take time out of your nighttime schedule to pray with her. There is something about a bedtime that makes daughters talk and talk and talk! Take advantage of this.

5. Every once-in-a-while either have your daughter's friends over for pizza or take them to a fun activity. Listen to them. You can learn a lot about your daughter from her friends!

ELTON, FATHER OF ESMEE

"Why stew about a trifle!"
Life Motto could have been:
"Que sera sera, whatever will be, will be…"

Elton was a careless man. He wove his webs to any length that happened to be easiest at the time. No two webs were ever the same. Elton's relationship with Esmee suffered because of his neglect. He just didn't care about her enough to go into the "inner room" of her life. He didn't talk to her about the gift Clotho gave her or about the promise God had given in regard to her future husband.

Elton's fatal flaw was that he didn't have a plan. He was an off-the-cuff kind of guy, flying by the seat of his pants. Life with him was never dull, but there was no structure to it. Neglect can be something as simple as failing to give proper attention to the performance of a task or responsibility. It includes the failure to notice that something is amiss and can be handled with correction, discipline, and teaching.

BIBLE STUDY:

"He who spares his rod hates his son (daughter), but he who loves him (her) disciplines him (her) promptly." Proverbs 13:24 NKJV

1. What does the Bible say about the man who neglects his child?

_____

2. Do you consistently correct your daughter?

_____

3. List some of the reasons you don't correct your daughter.

_____

_____

4. What motivates a father to correct his daughter?

_____

_____

"But if anyone does not provide for his own, and especially for those of his household, he has denied the faith and is worse than an unbeliever." 1 Timothy 5:8 NKJV

5. Rephrase what the Bible says about the man who does not provide guidance and protection for his daughter.

_____

_____

_____

If you have been neglectful or negligent in disciplining and correcting your daughter or planning the steps you will take as your daughter becomes a young woman, take heart! It is not too late. God says: *"If we confess our sins, he is faithful and just and will forgive us our sins and purify us from all unrighteousness. If we claim we have not sinned, we make him out to be a liar and his word has no place in our lives."* *(1 John 1:9-10 NIV)*

If this is a sin in your life, confess it to God, your Heavenly Father. Then, as you feel led, confess your sin to your daughter.

ACTIVITY:

Grab a calendar or planner and take time to think and plan topics you want to talk about with your daughter. Remember, failure to plan means planning to fail. The following topics are in the "inner room" of your daughter's life. Take time to get to know her!

1. **Faith:** Where is your daughter in her walk with the Lord?
2. **Modesty:** The manner in which she presents herself to men and to others in her clothing, words, and actions.
3. **Crushes versus Love:** The dangers of crushes and how to avoid them; in other words the importance of guarding her own heart. Discuss her perspective on true love and yours.

4. **Boys and Boyfriends:** Talk with her about her friendships with boys, and how and when your family will approach a more serious relationship with a young man.
5. **Marriage:** Talk about the qualifications of a husband. The "Silver Yardstick Letter" should help you define and articulate your views.
6. **Education:** What are her plans for her future education? What are her lifetime goals? Become a student of your daughter by finding her areas of interest.
7. **Money Management and Work Ethics:** Take time and look for opportunities to talk to her about how she manages her money. Also, diligently teach her how to do a good job on all the tasks she undertakes.
8. **Family Members and Siblings:** How does she get along with her brothers and sisters? How does she get along with you or your wife? This topic will be one that is always changing with new issues for you to iron out with her.
9. **Friends:** Explore with her the types of friends she chooses and which ones are good influences.
10. **Social Responsibility:** Teen years are a time of great introspection for young women. It is your responsibility to train your daughter to have a heart for helping others. Teach her to focus on others and look for someone to serve.

Griffin, Father of Gabriella

"But there may be a slip 'twixt cup and lip.
What happens if our daughters cannot fulfill the con-
ditions required?"

Life Motto: "Wait and See"

Griffin was a thoughtful man. This third weaver took "painstaking" care to weave each web to the exact measurements of the man for whom he was weaving the mantle. He then carefully compared the cloak to the measurements on the silver yardstick that accompanied him always. He was considered to be meticulous, thorough, conscientious, and exact by his fellow weavers.

The manner in which he wove garments, was the same manner in which he reared his daughter. Griffin cared enough to enter Gabriella's "inner room" and talk to her about things that were important to both of them. Griffin determined a measurement or plan for each of his garments, measured down to the "ell and inch" so it would fit perfectly. In the same way, he created a plan for training his daughter to guard her purity and also the choice of a life's mate.

BIBLE STUDY:

"The plans of the diligent lead to profit as surely as haste leads to poverty." Proverbs 21:5 NIV

1. Write the promise in this verse.

_____

_____

2. Write the warning.

_____

_____

3. What does it mean for you to be diligent in regard to training your daughter?

_____

_____

_____

Some synonyms would be: industrious, persevering, hardworking, and persistent.

4. What kind of (spiritual) profit would you like to see in your daughter's life?

_____

_____

_____

_____

Commit your work to the LORD, and your plans will be established." Proverbs 16:3 NKJV

The Exegeses Parallel Bible reads for the same verse,

"Roll your work unto Yah Veh and your fabrications are established."

Picture the rolling of your plans like a big ball into God's capable hands and through Him; they are established…it is a done deal! No matter what your method of fathering, take a moment to commit your time to the Lord through prayer. Roll your hopes, dreams and plans for your daughter right into Him and confidently rest on the fact that He is the establisher of His plans for her.

BIBLE STUDY:

Look up Psalm 112:1-2. Meditate on the benefits of passing down God's boundaries to your daughter. Record your thoughts here and discover that the benefits are for both you and her!

_____

_____

_____

_____

_____

_____

Chapter Five

THE THREE WEBS
"...weave on, then."

Dinah always worked in secret, ever peering out the window, so she would not miss the long-haired page in bright crimson clothing should he slip by and she not see him. The sheen of his fair hair dazzled her more than anyone else on whom her eyes had fallen. His face was all she thought of by day and dreamed of by night so that she often forgot how to ply[18] her needle or finger her lute. He was only a page, but in her fanciful mind she called him prince until she really believed him to be one. When she worked at the web she softly sang this sad song to herself, "It is for him—for him!"

Esmee laughed openly about her web, and her father often teased her about the one for whom it was intended. "Is that your prince?" or, "Is it for this one you weave?" he would ask. But, he never went with her into Esmee's inner room, so he never knew whether her weaving was done well or ill. And he never knew that

---

18. **Ply**, to diligently work with or handle skillfully.

she cut the web of one year's weaving and gave it away to the curly haired shepherd lad. He wore the cloak with jaunty grace at first, and Esmee spent long hours at the window watching him pass by all wrapped within its folds. But it soon grew soiled after awhile from his long tramps after his flocks of sheep over the dirt moors. After a time, Esmee saw other figures through the window who pleased her fancy, and she began another web. That web she gave to a student in cap and gown, the next to a troubadour[19] strolling past her window, and the next to a knight in armor who rode by one long, hot, idle summer day.

As the years went by, she scattered her favors to whoever called her sweetheart with vows of devotion, while Dinah remained faithful to the page alone.

Gabriella worked on, true to her promise. Then came a time when a face so noble and fair shone through her window so that she started back in a flutter.

She ran to her father and whispered breathlessly, "Oh, surely 'tis he! His eyes are so blue they fill all my dreams." But wise old Griffin answered her gently, "Does he measure up to the standard set by the sterling yardstick for a full grown prince to be?"

"No," she answered, sadly, "only to the measure of an ordinary man. But see how perfectly the mantle I've woven would fit him?"

---

19. **Troubadour**, a wandering musician or entertainer.

"No child; weave on, then," he said, kindly. "You have not yet reached the best you can do. Gabriella, you are still growing into the woman you will be. This is not the one that has been promised by God for you."

Chapter Five

DISCUSSION GUIDE

The Three Webs

"Then there came a time when a face shone so noble and fair through her window that she started back in a flutter."

After the three young girls were introduced to the loom, they each worked, in her way, on the special mantle she was to weave for the prince. How did each of the girls weave their garments?

ESMEE, DAUGHTER OF ELTON

"...Laughed openly about her web, and her father often teased her about the one for whom it was intended."

Nickname: *"Dream Weaver"*

1. Esmee laughed openly about her web. What does this tell you about how important she felt it was?

_____

_____

_____

_____

_____

_____

2. Elton never went into Esmee's inner room, so he didn't know about the woven quality of her web. Do you think this helped Esmee or hurt her?

_____

_____

Why?

_____

_____

_____

3. Esmee wove many a web for many a suitor. List them all here.

_____

_____

_____

4. These sad words sum up Esmee's young life: "she scattered her favors to whoever called her sweetheart with vows of devotion." Do you think the same results would have occurred if her father had taken a stronger role in her life? Explain your answer.

_____

_____

_____

_____

5. What do you think was the main thing Esmee did wrong? How could she have corrected it?

_____

_____

DINAH, DAUGHTER OF DEXTER

"…always worked in secret, ever peering out the window,"

Nickname: "Shame Weaver"

❧

1. Why do you think Dinah always worked in secret?

_____

_____

2. Write her reason for always looking out the window.

_____

_____

_____

3. What other duties did she neglect and why were they important?

_____

_____

_____

4. "He was only a page in her fanciful mind but she called him prince until she really believed him to be one." Do you think Dinah was deceiving herself?

_____

Have you ever done this to yourself? Describe the time here.

_____

_____

5. To whom alone did Dinah remain faithful?

_____

_____

6. In your opinion, what was the main thing Dinah did wrong? How could she have corrected it?

_____

_____

GABRIELLA, DAUGHTER OF GRIFFIN

"…worked on, true to her promise."
Nickname: "Weaver Extraordinaire"

⟨✕⟩

1. "Gabriella worked on, true to her promise." What does this reveal about her character?

_____

_____

2. When a fair and noble face shone through her window, what was her reaction?

_____

_____

3. Griffin asked if the young man measured up to the standard set by the sterling yardstick. In your family, what might be some of the measures of a worthy prince for you? Discuss this together.

_____

_____

_____

_____

4. When Gabriella measured this man he was only the measure of an "ordinary" man. How did Griffin encourage her to "weave on"?

_____

_____

5. What was the main thing Gabriella did right?

_____

Is there anything that she could have done to improve?

_____

_____

6. Of all three girls, with which one do you identify most? Why?

_____

_____

_____

Chapter Five

FATHER'S BIBLE STUDY

The Three Webs

"Catch for us the foxes, the little foxes that ruin the
vineyards, our vineyards that are in bloom."
(Song of Songs 2:15 NIV)

The three young girls busily worked on their mantles, each in her own way. One wove in secret, one laughed openly and did not perceive the preciousness of her web, and the last one wove on just as she had promised her father. Just as mistakes would show up in the fabric of the mantles they were weaving, so errors in their lives became evident. The choices two of them made revealed their lack of trust in their earthly fathers but even more importantly, their heavenly Father.

Can the same thing be said about your daughter? As you examine the fabric of her life, are you seeing evidence of her trusting in you? Of her trusting in her heavenly Father?

The following Bible study is the most important one in this book. It will help you determine if your daughter has received Christ as her Savior. Please do the Bible study with her. Look up the verses and answer the questions together.

BIBLE STUDY:

1. **1 John 1:8** Is anyone without sin?

_____

2. **Romans 3:12 and 23** According to these passages are your works good? Explain.

_____

Are you "good" enough to enter heaven?

_____

3. **Romans 5:8** How did God demonstrate His love for you?

_____

For whom did Christ die?

_____

4. **2 Corinthians 5:21** What was Christ made for you?

_____

Why?

_____

5. **Romans 6:23** According to this passage, what do you deserve?

_____

Through Christ what do you receive?

_____

6. Romans 10:9 and 10 What must you do to be saved?

_____

Explain the answer in your own words.

_____

_____

_____

_____

_____

Look up the following verses and ask your daughter if she has done these things in her life. Discuss them.

1. **Repent:** Luke 13:3; Mark 1:15
2. **Confess:** 1John 1:9; Romans 10:9
3. **Believe:** Acts 16:31; Hebrews 11:6
4. **Decide:** 2 Corinthians 6:1-2; Joshua 24:14-16

If your daughter has never before confessed her sin, repented and asked Jesus to become her Savior, lead her through this process. She may have heard this process many times before, but this may be the day she truly understands it! If she accepts Christ as her Savior today, know that "*there is rejoicing in the presence of the angels over one sinner who repents.!*" *(Luke 15:10 NIV)*

Father, make sure your daughter has entrusted her life to you. She should not only place herself under her heavenly

Father's protection, but she must also trust you enough to allow you to protect her here on earth. Is she willing to place her heart in your hands? Is she willing to give you the key to her heart for safe keeping? The following questions will help you to really discover your daughter's heart. You have the responsibility and the privilege of learning about your daughter and finding out if she really has given her trust to you. *"Be sure you know the condition of your flocks (children), give special attention to your herds (family)."* *(Proverbs 27:23 NIV)*

Ask your daughter these questions and discuss her answers:

1. Do you feel like you make mistakes?
2. Are there areas in your life where you could use my input?
3. Are you willing to follow my guidance?
4. Are you willing for me to give you advice on your choice of friends, books, and entertainment?
5. Will you allow me to talk to you about what is and isn't modest clothing? Are you willing to modify the choices of the clothing you pick according to what I believe is appropriate?
6. Do you understand that the guidelines we have set up regarding relationships with young men, and ultimately finding a husband, are for your protection? Are you willing to submit to our rules about this?
7. Do you trust me enough to bring to my attention any young men who are interested in you?
8. When you do not agree with my judgments, are you still going to be obedient to my decisions? Why?
9. Will you allow me to be involved with your life and ask you tough questions about relationships, activities, and attitudes?
10. Are you willing to believe I have your best interest at heart even though it may not seem like it at the time?

ACTIVITY:

Father, please notice how Griffin spoke to his daughter reassuring her that he had only her good at heart. In this activity you will write a pledge to your daughter about this.

1. Take time to explain in a letter why your daughter can always trust you.
   Four areas of trust to include in your letter are:
   • You will pray for her and God's choice for her life partner.
   • You will teach her the Lord's principles of life.
   • You will protect her from men that are not qualified.
   • You always have her best interest at heart.

2. Plan to give your daughter the letter during your time together. She may want to frame it or put it in her hope chest.

THE THREE PRINCES

"At last it came to pass, as it was promised by God."

Along time passed, then another knight appeared in Gabriella's window, a knight as gallant as Sir Lancelot:

> *"His broad clear brow in sunlight glowed.*
> *On burnished hooves his war-horse trod*
> *From underneath his helmet flowed,*
> *His coal black curls, as on he rode*
> *As he rode down to Camelot."*

So noble was he that Gabriella felt sure that he was the one destined to wear her mantle. She went to her father, Griffin, saying, "He has asked me for the robe, and measured by the silver yardstick, it would fit him faultlessly, as the falcon's feathers fit the falcon."

Griffin laid the yardstick against the web. "No." he said. "This is only the size of a knight. It lacks a hand-breadth[20] yet of the measure of a prince."

---

20. **Handbreadth,** an old unit of measure of the distance between one hand spread open.

Gabriella hesitated, half pouting, till her father reminded her, "I am an old man, knowing far more of the world and its ways than you, my daughter. Have I ever deceived you? Have I ever had aught[21] but your good at heart? Have patience a little longer. Another year and you will be able to fashion a still larger web."

At last it came to pass, as it was promised by God. A prince came riding by to ask for Dinah's hand. Dexter said, "Now I will lead you into the inner room and teach you how to use Clotho's wonderful gift. With me for your teacher you will certainly make no mistakes!"

When they came into the inner room there stood only the empty loom from which the golden warp had been clipped.

"What happened?" Dexter demanded, angrily. Dinah, braving his ill humor, said defiantly, "You are too late. Because I was afraid of your scorn at what you called my childish foolishness, I wove in secret, and when my prince came by long ago I gave it to him. Look, he is standing just outside my window."

The astonished Dexter turned in rage and saw the longhaired page clad in the mantle, which Dinah had woven in secret. He tore it angrily from the youth and demanded she should give it to the prince who waited to claim it, but the prince would have none of it. The mantle

---

21. **Aught**, anything.

was too small in size to fit his royal shoulders and had been defiled when worn by a common page. With one look of disdain, the prince rode away not even retrieving out of his traveling pack the wedding gown that he had carefully fashioned for her.

Stripped of the robe her own fancy had woven around him, the page stood shorn[22] before her. It was as if a veil had been torn away from her eyes, and she no longer saw him as her fond dreams had painted him. She saw him for what he really was in all his unworthiness. The cloth of gold, which was her maiden-love, and the rosy dreams she had woven into it to make the mantle of a high ideal lay in tattered shreds at her feet.

When she compared the prince to the page, she saw the dreadful mistake she had made and the opportunity she had lost. She covered her face with her hands and cried out to Dexter, "It is your fault! You should not have laughed at my childish questions with scorn. You drove me to weave in ignorance and in secret!" But all her upbraidings[23] were too late. As her father was warned by Clotho on the day of her birth, Dinah's heart was as broken and shattered as the mirror of the Lady of Shalott.

That very same day there came a prince to Elton, asking for his daughter. He called her from the garden gaily, "Bring forth your mantle now, Esmee. Surely it must be a good one after all these years of weaving at your own sweet will."

---

22. **Shorn**, to be sheared. Like the wool is shorn from a sheep.
23. **Upbraiding**, to reprove or reproach.

She brought it forth, but when Elton saw its tiny size he was aghast. When he demanded the reason, she confessed with tears that she had no more of the golden warp that was part of Clotho's blessed gift. She had squandered that maiden-love over years to make the mantles she had so thoughtlessly given to the shepherd lad, the troubadour, the student and the knight. This was all she had left to give.

"Well," said her father, at length, "'tis only what many others have done in the wanton[24] foolishness of youth. But, perchance when the prince sees how fair you are, and how sweetly you do sing with the lute, he may overlook the paltriness of your offering. Take your mantle to him."

When she had laid it before the prince he cast only one glance at it, so small it was, so meager of gold thread, so unmeet for a true prince's wearing. Then he looked sorrowfully into the depths of her beautiful eyes, gathered up the intricately embroidered wedding gown he had made especially as a wedding gift for his bride and turned away. The gaze of the promised prince burned into her very soul and revealed to her all that she had lost forevermore.

Esmee cried out to her father with pitiful sobs that set his heartstrings a quiver: "It is your fault! Why didn't you warn me what a precious gift was the golden warp Clotho gave me? Why did you say to me, 'Is this the lad? Is that the lad?' Till I looked only at the village churls[25] and wove my web to fit their unworthy shoulders and forgot how high was the stature of my promised prince."

---

24. **Wanton**, unrestrained, playful, licentious manner.
25. **Churls**, ill-natured peasants.

Then hiding her face, she ran away. As her father was warned on the day of Esmee's birth, her heart broke like the shattered mirror of the Lady of Shalott.

Then came a prince to Gabriella. After studying her for a moment, he handed her a beautifully embroidered gown which he had spent years carefully embroidering and designing for his future bride. The threads that created the intricate floral pattern were of brilliant gold. Holding the gown up to her, Gabriella found that it would fit her perfectly. Shyly she set the gown gently aside. Gabriella knew that she had reached the moment she had waited and prepared for all her life. All blushing and aflutter, she clipped the threads that held the golden web of her maiden-love, through which ran all her happy girlish daydreams, and let him take it from her. Glancing up shyly, she saw that it fit him as perfectly as a falcon's feathers fit a falcon.

Old Griffin, stretching out his hands, said, "Dear child, because even in childhood days you always kept in view the silver yardstick as I asked you, because no single strand of all the golden warp that Clotho gave you was squandered on another, because you waited till your woman's fingers made the best that lay within a woman's heart, all happiness will be yours! Receive it as your perfect crown!"

So with her father's blessing upon her, Gabriella rode away beside her prince; and ever after, all her life was crowned with happiness as the Lord had promised on the day of her birth.

Chapter Six

DISCUSSION GUIDE

The Three Princes

"At last it came to pass, as it was promised by God,
A prince came riding by …"

DINAH'S PRINCE

"Because I was afraid of your scorn…I wove in secret."
Nickname: "Shame Weaver"

1. Finally, Dinah's prince came riding by to ask her for her hand in marriage. What action did Dexter finally take?

   _____

   _____

2. Describe the attitude Dexter had when he led his daughter into the inner room.

   _____

   _____

3. Can you suggest a better way he should have acted?

   _____

   _____

4. Describe his reaction when he found out the golden loom was empty.

_____

_____

5. Dinah, braving his ill-humor said defiantly, "You are too late! Because I was afraid of your scorn...I wove in secret." In your opinion, did she have a *right* to weave in secret because she feared her father's scorn? Explain.

_____

_____

6. Who was the one whom Dinah called her "prince"?

_____

Describe what Dexter did to the mantle.

_____

_____

7. What reasons did the prince give for refusing to wear her cloak before he rode away?

_____

_____

_____

8. "It was as if a veil had been torn away from her eyes…" What happened to Dinah's perception of *her* prince after the cloak was taken from him?

_____

_____

9. Whom did she blame for her mistake?

_____

10. The story says, "Her heart was as broken and shattered as the mirror of the Lady of Shalott." What do you think happened to Dinah's life? Complete her story on the following lines.

_____

_____

_____

_____

_____

_____

_____

_____

_____

_____

_____

ESMEE'S PRINCE

" I laughed openly about my web."
Nickname: *"Dream Weaver"*

1. When Esmee's prince came riding by to ask for her hand, Elton told her to bring her mantle out. He was anticipating it to be a "goodly one" since she had been working on it a long time. What was Elton's reaction to the mantle that she brought out? Explain.

_____

_____

_____

_____

_____

2. What was the reason she gave for the small mantle?

_____

_____

_____

_____

_____

FOOD FOR THOUGHT:
Four mantles for regular men would make one mantle for a prince!

---

3. Describe Elton's solution to his daughter's plight.

_____

_____

4. Explain the prince's reaction to the small mantle.

_____

_____

Did Esmee's beauty make up for the gift that was
intended for him?

_____

_____

5. The story says, "Her heart was as broken and shattered as the mirror of the Lady of Shalott." What do
you think happened to Esmee's life? Complete her
story.

_____

_____

_____

_____

_____

_____

_____

_____

_____

_____

Gabriella's Prince

"I worked on, true to my promise."
Nickname: "Weaver Extraordinaire"

❧

1. "Then came a prince to Gabriella." The princes of the other two girls came to their fathers to ask for the mantle. Speculate on what might have been the difference between the three girls that caused Gabriella's prince to go directly to her.

2. "...she clipped the threads that held the golden web ..." It was not her father who clipped the thread, but rather Gabriella. What does this mean?

3. Griffin had promised her that the mantle she wove for her promised prince would fit him "as perfectly as a falcon's feathers fit a falcon." Did the mantle fit the prince?

4. How could this be applied to your own life? Discuss this together.

_____

_____

_____

5. What was Griffin's reaction to the events taking place? Record what he said.

_____

_____

_____

_____

6. Does this sound like a blessing to you?

_____

7. According to old Griffin, what were the reasons Gabriella had not faltered and given her mantle away before the proper time?

_____

_____

_____

_____

8. Is this something you can picture your father saying to you? Why or why not?

_____

_____

"Gabriella rode away beside her prince; and ever after, all her life was crowned with happiness as the Lord had promised on the day of her birth." Can you write the ending to Gabriella's life or do you feel that it is complete? Write your opinion on what you believe the ending would be.

Gabriella's Story

"and ever after, all her life was crowned with happiness as the Lord had promised on the day of her birth."

_____

_____

_____

_____

_____

_____

_____

_____

_____

_____

_____

Chapter Six
FATHER'S BIBLE STUDY
The Three Princes

"At last it came to pass, as it was promised by God. A prince came riding by …"

From the day of the daughters' births, the fathers set into motion the conclusion of the story by their words and deeds (or lack of them!). Two of the girls' hearts were as broken as the Lady of Shalott's and one *"rode away beside her prince; and ever after, all her life was crowned with happiness as the Lord had promised on the day of her birth."* What the fathers sowed, their daughters reaped. In this final study, we will examine more closely the law of sowing and reaping.

> *"Do not be deceived; God is not mocked, for whatever a man sows, that he will also reap. For he who sows to his own flesh will from the flesh reap corruption; but he who sows to the Spirit will from the Spirit reap eternal life. And let us not grow weary in well doing, for in due season we shall reap, if we do not lose heart. So then, as we have opportunity, let us do good to all men, and especially to those who are of the household of faith."* Galatians 6:7-10 NKJV

Dinah's Prince

"...always worked in secret, ever peering out the window,"

Nickname: "Shame Weaver"

Dexter sowed the seeds of harshness, rigidity and legalism into Dinah's life. Dinah allowed the seed of bitterness and rebellion to take root and flourish, and she reaped heartache.

Bible Study:

Read the following verses to discover what they say about:

Dinah's life

Proverbs 17: 11 _____

1 Samuel 15:23a_____

God's solution

Hebrews 12:14-15 _____

Ephesians 6:1-4 _____

Dexter's life

Deuteronomy 4:9; 11:19 _____

Has your daughter been rebellious and refused to submit to the rules that you have given for her own protection? Don't give up! Place the emphasis on your love for her and labor to develop your relationship with her.

That was Christ's method with us. *"But God demonstrates His own love for us in this: while we were still sinners Christ died for us." (Romans 5:8 NIV)* He acted upon His love by dying on the cross for us even while we were still sinners. He died for your rebellious daughter as well and loves her even more than you do.

ESMEE'S PRINCE

"...laughed openly about her web, and her father often teased her about the one for whom it was intended"

Nickname: "Dream Weaver"

Elton sowed the seeds of neglect, ignorance, and foolishness into Esmee's life. From these seeds, promiscuity sprouted and became a way of life for her. The seeds given her contained no discernment and Esmee reaped heartache.

BIBLE STUDY:

Read the following verses to discover what they say about:

Esmee's life

Jeremiah 6:15a (RSV) _____

Proverbs 11:22 _____

Proverbs 3:7-8 Proverbs 25:28 _____

God's Solution

    Ephesians 4:32   _____

Elton's life

    Mattthew 18:6   _____

ACTIVITY:

If your daughter is or has been promiscuous, do not despair! God knows what has happened in her life and wants to restore her. No matter where you are on your journey as a father, Jesus is the answer to healing and restoring her life. Pray for your daughter and trust Him as you give her to His perfect will and plan for her life.

GABRIELLA'S PRINCE

"...worked on, true to her promise."
Nickname: "Weaver Extraordinaire"

Griffin sowed seeds of love, trust, and consistency. Gabriella allowed the good seeds to take root. They bore a harvest of mutual trust, love and obedience. Gabriella reaped her promised reward and garnered a lifetime of joy.

BIBLE STUDY:

Read the following verses and discover what they say about:

Gabriella's life

Ephesians 6:1-3 _____

James 1:3-4 (TLB) _____

Hebrews 12:11 _____

Proverbs 3:5-6 _____

Proverbs 4: 26-27 _____

Psalm 101:1-4 _____

Griffin's life

Psalm 112:1-2 _____

ACTIVITY:

Congratulations Father! You have completed *The Three Weavers Plus Companion Guide* with your daughter. Following are suggestions of ways for commemorating the time you had together and your mutual trust.

Purchase a piece of jewelry for your daughter to wear to serve as a visible reminder of her pledge to wait to give herself until she is married to the " prince" God has chosen for her. It will also be a symbol of your love for her as she faces conflict, challenges and change. It will remind her how precious she is to you and how deeply you care.

Most of all, it will be a continuous reminder of the plan and promise God has for her life.

Plan a special evening when you and your wife take her out for a meal. Give her the gift at dessert. It will be a memory she will always treasure!

We gave our daughter a ring that had two rubies and one diamond in it. The design signified the relationship she would wait for and someday have. Her husband and herself with God in the middle based on the verse: *"A cord of three strands is not quickly broken." (Ecclesiastics 4:12 NIV)*

Here are some other ideas. Be sensitive to your daughter's taste in jewelry.

- Cross necklace
- Heart locket
- Purity ring
- Wristwatch
- Ring (pearl, precious stone, signet)

The following poem on page 129 can be read at your daughter's Purity Celebration.

PURITY RING

Let this ring now ever be
A symbol of your purity,
An emblem of your love for Me.
For I am He Who leadeth thee,
Who gave My life upon the tree,
And all this for your purity.
And when your eyes behold and see
This ring,
This ring of purity,
Remember this,
The promise that you made to Me,
For I own every minute of each hour.
Your future is secure within My power.
And when I tell you, "Look and see
The one whom I prepared for thee,"
Then you will see.
You'll know why I preserved your purity
And kept you safe from all the worldly,
And why I drew you unto me.

RESOURCES

Hope Chests:

Hope Chest Legacy
P.O. Box 1398
Littlerock, CA 93543
(888) 554-7292

Purity Jewelry:

AIM Enterprises (Articles Inspiring Maturity)
507 Grace - Stockholm
Aurora, NE 68818
(402) 737-3312
www.aim4theheart.com

> *This family owned company has a unique "Key To My Heart" ring. Included in this set are a heart shaped ring with a key hole in the center, tie-tack/lapel pin for the father in the shape of a key, and a covenant of purity and protection for the daughter and parents to sign. The key to his daughter's heart is kept until her wedding day when the father will pin it to the groom's lapel before giving his daughter to him symbolically transferring protection and ownership of her heart to her husband.*

Lord's Fine Jewelry
P.O. Box 486
Piedmont, OK 73078
(405) 373-2877

Genesis Christian Jewelry
Factory 79 Inc.
San Diego, CA 92192-2839
(800) 677-0832
www.factory79.com

Purity Designs
22606 South 4190 Road
Claremore, OK 74017
(918) 343-6224
www.purityring.com

Samaritan Arts Jewelry
2427 I-40 West
Amarillo, TX 79109
(800) 658-6148
www.christianjewelryusa.com

ChristianRings.Com
2882 Los Gatos Drive
Belleair Bluffs, Florida 33770
(877) 347-4764
www.christianrings.com

ORDERING INFORMATION

For more information or to place an order, please contact:

Pumpkin Seed Press LLC
43668 355th Ave.
Humphrey, NE 68642
(877) 923-1682
www.pumpkinseedpress.net

Also available from Pumpkin Seed Press LLC,

The Companion Guide to Beautiful Girlhood

This book was written for young girls between the ages of 9 and 15 years. It is based on the classic book, *Beautiful Girlhood*, written by Mabel Hale in 1940, and revised by Karen Andreola. This 32 week character study is a delightful way to build precious memories, and strong character while helping young girls to make the transition into womanhood. Used extensively for individual and group Mother/Daughter Bible Studies.

Winsome Womanhood Daybreak   Journal Edition

Winsome Womanhood was crafted for young women between the ages of 12 and 16. The original text was first published in 1900 by Margaret E. Sangster. This classic volume yields the common sense and godly wisdom of a woman who really understood women. The Journal Edition makes it an ideal tool for molding, guiding, and getting to know young women in the daybreak of their lives. A special emphasis is placed on management of home and life.

Tea Time Products

Are you searching for a way to make the time spent with your daughter special? Take a look online at Pumpkin Seed's Tea Time Products! We carry a large assortment of teacups, teapots, and teas to create lasting memories while you mentor your daughters. **www.pumpkinseedpress.net**.

Pumpkin Seed
P R E S S